We Did It

Written by Sofia Koval

Illustrated by Sherri White

Consonant *Dd* /d/

and	did
dab	dip
Dad	sad

Consonant *Kk* /k/

Kat
Kip
kit

High-Frequency Words

are	my	that
look	of	we

Look, Kat and Kip!

Look at my kit!

We tap and tap.

Look at that!

We dip in cans of tan.

Dad can dab.

We are not sad!